A Season Of Mercy

A Season Of Mercy

Mercy

MARTHA MANNING

Illustrations by Elizabeth J. French

AVE MARIA PRESS
Notre Dame, Indiana 46556

About the author:

A Season of Mercy is Martha Manning's first book. A clinical psychologist with a private practice, Manning is also on the faculty of George Mason University. She is a graduate of the University of Maryland, earned her Master's and Ph.D. degrees from Catholic University of America and was a post-doctoral fellow at Harvard University Medical School.

Excerpt from *The Collected Poems of Thomas Merton* copyright © 1977 by The Abbey of Gethsemani, Inc. and The Trustees of the Merton Legacy Trust. Published by New Directions. All rights reserved.

© 1988 by Ave Maria Press, Notre Dame, Indiana 46556

International Standard Book Number: 0-87793-379-0

Library of Congress Catalog Card Number: 88-70574

Printed and bound in the United States of America.

For Brian and Keara—
through them I know the mercy of God in joy,
and for my lost children—
through them I know the mercy of God in sorrow.

*W*ho is more little, who is more poor, than the helpless man who lies asleep in his bed without awareness and without defense? Who is more trusting than he who must entrust himself each night to sleep? What is the reward of his trust? Gentleness comes to him when he is most helpless and awakens him, refreshed, beginning to be made whole. Love takes him by the hand and opens to him the doors of another life, another day. . . . When the helpless one awakens strong at the voice of mercy, it is as if Life his Sister. . . were to stand over him and invite him with unutterable sweetness to be awake and to live. This is what it means to recognize . . . Sophia.

Sophia is the mercy of God in us. She is the tenderness with which the infinitely mysterious power of pardon turns the darkness of our sins into the light of grace. She is the inexhaustible fountain of kindness and would almost seem to be, in herself, all mercy.

Thomas Merton
''Hagia Sophia''
Emblems of a Season of Fury

Sophia came to her one night.

She came to deliver her
 from the darkness of the night
 and the darker nights to come.

She did not recognize Sophia
 but in some ways she had always known her . . .
  in moments
  in fragments
  in glimpses.

8

Sophia came to her when she felt alone.
Alone with a baby inside
a baby who couldn't wait.

A baby who started in a mother
who waited eight years to feel ready.

A baby who began in a mother
who was readier in her heart
than she was in her body.

A baby who is now gone.

She was ill when she found she was pregnant
ill with a flu that lingered
and turned to pneumonia.

This pregnancy was so different from the first.

It turned the mother upside down
and shook her so hard
she feared she would never be the same again.

Nothing worked right
she had difficulty breathing
she forgot how to sleep
she became enemies with food.

She clutched frantically
        at her sense of control
        of what was real.

        But they were hard things to hold.

At times it seemed
        that the baby's well-being
        and hers were mutually exclusive

        and that day by day
                as the baby grew inside her
                she felt herself diminished.

She grew more distant
from the people who loved her.

It was as if
a glass partition
separated them.
She could see them
their arms outstretched to comfort her.
She could hear the soothing tones
but their voices were muffled
and the words came from a language
she had known once
but could not now understand.

All the things
that had helped before
seemed useless now.

And as she discarded them one by one
she felt her despair grow
with the child inside.

She had recently come
to a new understanding
of a higher power
a loving God.

A God who in the images
of father and mother
was above all
gentle and compassionate
and she was just learning
how to pray to this God.

Her prayers before had always been
    in groups of people
    or in the half prayer, half blasphemous exclamations
    she had been saying since her adolescence
    —prayers for immediate and divine intervention
        ''Jesus, let me get to this meeting on time'' or
        ''God, just let me get through this lecture without
            looking like a fool.''

Prayers were things
    said with others
    or alone under pressure.

Once they were said, they were over.
    Cross them off the list of things to do.
        There was no exploration
           and no listening.

But she had never felt so sick and helpless in her life
and she felt it might be time
to pray in a different way.

She prayed first to the more familiar image
of God as a father.

She prayed that she wasn't sure
how much more sleeplessness
and breathlessness and nausea
she could take.

She admitted her vulnerability
and asked for compassion.

And she waited.

She waited
        for comfort
        for relief
        for changes in her body
                —and none came.

God is not a father.

That image is a lie.

She knew about good fathers
  she had one
  she lived with another.

She remembered
  the way her father suffered
      at the pain of his children
  and how even in their adulthood
      he ached for them
          as they struggled through difficult times.

She had ample opportunity
  to see her husband
      as a joyful, gentle father with their daughter.

She knew
  the way he hovered and suffered
  trying to get medicine down the throat
  of a feverish and resistant little girl.

She remembered him
  rocking and singing
  to a child too sick to sleep.

No, she knew good fathers.
  She knew them very well
      and God was not one of them.

Then she remembered an image of God
    which was less familiar to her
    but one which she welcomed when she first heard it.
      God as nurturing, gentle mother.

This was it.

Perhaps it would take a woman
    to understand what she was experiencing.

She prayed to God as her mother.
    She told Her of the fears for her baby
      the high fevers
      the medications
      the weakness.

She begged Her to make her a stronger mother
    so that her body could sustain this baby.

She knew what to expect.
    She knew it from her experience of her own mother
    and from herself as a mother.

She remembered her mother's soothing words of comfort
    as she lay in bed with high fevers.

She could feel
        the fresh clean sheets
        the cool cloths on her forehead
        the spoonfuls of crushed ice.

And she knew how it felt
    to see her child suffer
        a slight at school
        an invisible ache
        a real illness.

She knew that she
    would exchange her strength and health
    for her child's suffering
        in a second
        if she could.

She prayed to God her mother
    to make her healthy
    so that she could give her strength
        to this new child.

But there was
    no change
    no answer.

God is not a mother.

The image is a fantasy
    another lie.

She stopped believing
before she had even really started.

God could stop the sickness.
God could help.

It would be so simple.

But God didn't.

Why was this happening?

What had she done to deserve this?

She had some sense of an answer
several days later
in the obstetrician's office.

After hearing him warn
    that it could be too early
    to hear the baby's heartbeat
        they tried it anyway.

It was like tuning in to a radio station
    hundreds of miles away
        static and distant.

But then she could hear her own heartbeat
    rhythmic
    whooshing
    slow.

And then gradually
    she began to distinguish another sound.

She heard it before anyone else.

She and the doctor
    looked up at each other
    nodded and smiled.

There it was—
    the baby's heartbeat
        strong and fast
            sounding just like her daughter's
            like a little rabbit's.

That was her child.

Now she knew
    that her baby was fine
        despite the way she felt.

And she grudgingly acknowledged to herself
    that this could be
        God's answer to her questions.

The baby was alright.

She could withstand the suffering
    for a few more weeks.

It would be over soon.

But things got worse.

    She grew weaker
        was losing sleep and weight
        was prone to bouts of despair and crying
        that came over her
        quickly and cruelly.

One evening she lay on her bed
    with sweats and chills
    feeling sick and weak
        and losing the hope
        that she would ever feel different.

    As she closed her eyes to try to sleep
        the tears began to sting
        and fall down her cheeks

and she tried to recall
        an image
            that had always helped
                to comfort
                and calm her.

*I*t was a scene from her childhood—
   her grandparents' beach house.

It was a typical New England beach
      whose terrain often changed radically
         with the seasons and the years.

      She remembered
            that as a child
            she arrived at the beach
                  late at night
                  too late to see what the beach looked like that year.

      She always woke very early the next morning
            ran to the sea wall
            and scanned the beach for changes.

She loved that scene
      and it brought her a gentle peace
      in the times she let herself imagine it.

It came to her differently this time
      as she lay there exhausted
      in the space between awake and asleep.

There were two people in the scene this time,

> herself
> and an old woman in a yellow slicker
> walking along the beach.

She had never seen the woman before, and yet
there was so much about her that was familiar

> her white-blonde hair was pulled back
> with wisps falling around her face

> and her hands were like her mother's
> —artist's hands.

It was strange.
> She looked a little like
> > her mother
> > her husband's mother

> a little like
> > her grandmothers

all in a diffuse way that could not fit words.

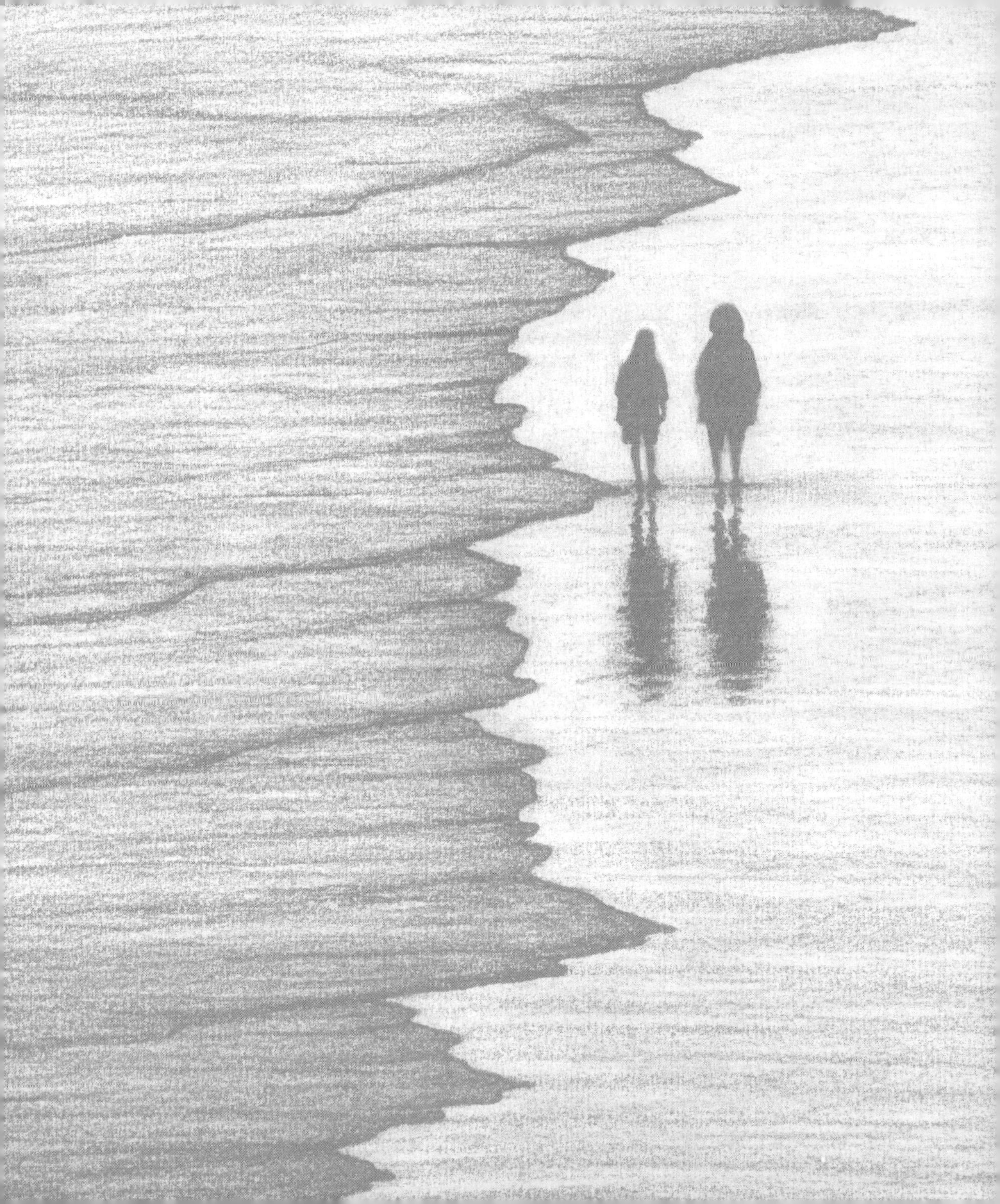

The old woman seemed to know her.
    She smiled and greeted her by name.

Puzzled she asked:
    "How do you know my name?"

The old woman laughed and replied,
    "Child, see that lighthouse?"

Of course she saw the lighthouse—
    Minot Light.
    She loved that lighthouse.

    At night she loved to sit on the sea wall
        hypnotized by the rhythm of its blinking light.

    When she was a little girl,
    her mother told her
        that it spelled out in code
        the words "I love you."

    As an adult she wasn't sure
        if that was really true
        but it was one of those things she didn't really want to
            know the truth about

    just in case it spelled something else
        or worse
        —nothing at all.

"Yes," she replied,
    "I've known the lighthouse
      all my life."

"Well, child, I'm Sophia
    the keeper of the lighthouse.
        I've known you all of your life."

As she tried to figure that out
    the old woman motioned her toward the shore
        held out her hand
        and said, "Let's walk."

They walked
    slowly and silently
        watching the water
        watching the beach.

In the silence
    she was overcome with sadness
        and began to cry.

The old woman stopped walking
    and asked why she was crying.

She began to sob
    and said,
        I'm so sick
            and scared.

    I feel so alone
        and I'm not strong anymore.

    I don't understand
        what's happening to me.

    I can't make it better
        and no one else can either.

The old woman smiled at her and said,
"Child, look closely at the beach.
Has it always looked like this?"

She was puzzled
—why would the lighthouse keeper
ask such a stupid question?

But she tried to respond.
"No, it's never the same.
It's always different."

"How is it different?"

"Well, it differs
with the seasons
with the years."

"Tell me about the differences."

"When the winter has been gentle
    the sand is so clear and smooth
    you can see the crabs scurry along the beach.

"When the winter has been harsh
    it is littered with thousands
    of rocks and shells
        and it takes all summer to toughen the bottoms of your
        feet so that you can finally walk barefoot.

"Some storms bring
    seaweed
    jellyfish
    junk

"and some of the storms
    wreck the boats
    and the moorings
    close to the shore.

"It's always different.
    That's why I like it."

"Tell me about the storms," said the old woman.

"They're fierce.
      The ocean goes wild
            and its power is
                  awesome
                  terrible

            but at the same time
                  beautiful.

"I loved watching the storms

            from the sea wall
            standing barefoot
            with a slicker over my bathing suit.

"My grandmother would call to me
            to come inside
            and watch behind the safety of the picture window.

"But she didn't understand
            I was safe on the sea wall.

            "It was exhilarating
            to be in the middle of it all
                  in danger
                  and in safety
                        at the same time."

"Well child," the old woman said,
   "the beach has been through
      gentle and fierce weather.

"It changes constantly,
     but it is always here.

    No matter what happens to it,
      every year
        the ocean
       and the beach
         are here for you.

"Do you understand?"

The young woman wasn't sure.
What was there to understand?

As she hesitated,
    the old woman asked another question.

"Tell me about the beach house.
    Has it always been the same?"

        "Oh, no. This is the fourth house I've known since I was a
            child."

"What happened to the houses?"

        "They were destroyed
            in hurricanes
            and blizzards.

        "But my grandparents always rebuilt them.

        "This fourth house was designed
            in a different way.

        "The other houses were destroyed
            by the force of water rushing through them.

"The new house was made
in two sections
connected
by a glass hallway.

"It was designed
so that in a bad storm
the ocean could have a way
to rush through it
without doing any major damage."

"What do you think of this house?"

"At first I did not like it at all.

It was so different from the houses of my childhood.
It's not a traditional New England beach house.

But it really is the most creative of all the houses.
It's also withstood some very hard winters."

"Yes it has," answered the old woman.
"Now do you understand?"

"What is this woman trying to tell me?"
thought the younger woman.

"Why doesn't she just come out and say
what she wants me to know
instead of playing this game with me?"

*T*hey walked on farther.
The old woman bent over
    and picked up something nestled in the rocks.

    She held it open in her hand
        for the young woman to see.

    It was a piece of glass
        smooth
        green
        opaque.

    As children they called it sea glass
        and competed with each other
        to see who could find the most beautiful pieces.

"Child, what is this?"

    "It's sea glass."
        The young woman answered impatiently.

"And how does it become sea glass?"

    "A bottle of glass breaks on the beach
        and then the sea
        and the rocks
        and the sand
            wear down the jagged edges
            take away the shine
            and put a crystal texture on it."

"I want you to understand about sea glass."

"What's to understand?
     I already told you what I know."

"Here, I want you to hold it
     rub your fingers around the edges
     feel it against your cheek."

The young woman explored the piece of glass.
     It was cool in her hand
     and the edges were curved and smooth.

"Okay," she said
    and tried to hand it back.

        The old woman laughed and said,
        "Child, you've only begun to know this glass."

She placed it back in the young woman's hand again and said,
    Look at it
    smell it
    taste it.

She looked at it closely
    and saw the different textures of green.

She held it up to the sky
    and watched the colors play
        with the glass and the water.

She saw ridges
    places where the glass was more worn than others.

She smelled the glass.
    It smelled like
        air
        salt
        sand
        water
            all at the same time.

Then she put the glass to her tongue
        and tasted it
        and instantly felt
        that she'd been engulfed by a wave of sorrow.

"What does it taste like, child?" asked the old woman
        looking directly into her eyes.

The young woman began to weep and answered,
        "It tastes like tears."

The old woman put her arms around her
        and held her close.

And she said softly in her ear,
        "Yes child, that's the sea
                that's the sea.

        "Do you understand now?"

She still wasn't sure she understood
        but she was beginning to know
                that the old woman
                        was telling her something important.

They stood in silence for several moments.

Then the old woman said,
    "There is something I want to tell you
    that you will need to remember.

    "Listen to me carefully
    and keep this with you:

    "This is a season . . . and all seasons pass."

Then the old woman said,
    "It's time for me to go now."

The younger woman
    grabbed her hand,
    pleading:
        "Please don't leave me alone."

The old woman laughed again and answered,
    "Child, just because you feel alone
        doesn't mean you are alone.

    I have known you always
        and now you know me.
            You can never be alone."

"But where are you going?
    Where can I look for you?"

"Look inside yourself
    and look all around you."

"Yes, but where can I find *You?*"

"You aren't listening to me.
   Look inside you
   look around you
      and if you forget where to look
         you can always look toward the lighthouse
         and let the light guide you."

The young woman began to protest
   with another question,
      "But I don't underst . . ."

"Child, you don't have to think about it.
   Just let it happen."

She ran her hands across the young woman's cheeks
   and wiped away her tears.

Then she kissed her forehead
   turned
      and walked slowly toward the light.

*T*he young woman opened her eyes
aware of being in her own room.

She drifted safely into sleep
sure that the lighthouse keeper's message
meant that the suffering
was almost over.

But things got harder.

In moments of despair
    she turned to her memory of Sophia
        the lighthouse woman
        and it gave her comfort.

    She repeated over and over to herself
        like a mantra,
           "This is a season . . . and all seasons pass."

And then
    one week after they heard the baby's heartbeat
        it was gone.

She saw her child
on the sonogram screen
its head
its feet.

But there was no heartbeat
no growth
no life.

The fragile threads
that had bound them together in life
had broken.

How did it happen?

Did the connection unravel
        slowly
        gradually?

Or did the threads
        break suddenly
        in one violent snap?

How could it happen without her knowing it?

But none of that really mattered now
        because her baby was dead.

God had answered her prayers
    to end the suffering
        by taking away the baby.

That's not what she asked for.
        God didn't even get her order right.

*P*eople immediately began to tell her
about the mercy of miscarriages.

Mercy???

"Don't talk to me about God's mercy," she thought.

"I asked for mercy
and I got pain.

"So I asked again for mercy
and I got more pain.

"So I asked again for mercy
and now my baby is gone.

There is no merciful God.

Life is fragile
and the world is random and callous."

The surgery was scheduled for eight hours later.
She and her husband had to wait several hours
    outside the surgical suite
    until all the scheduled surgeries were completed.

As she waited with her husband
    watching the stretchers pass
    in and out of surgery
        she felt empty
        and numb. . . .

But she felt something else.

She felt how perfectly her hand fit her husband's.
They must have held hands for three hours
as they sat in silence.

In a moment of such fragility
she felt the strength of their love
and it helped to fill the emptiness
and give her comfort.

Mercy.

He helped her change into her hospital gown.
   Piece by piece
      she offered up the parts of herself
     to him for safekeeping
       her coat
       her clothes
       her watch
       her rings
       her huge purse stuffed with
         books
         grocery lists
         pieces of poems
         notes to herself.

By the time she was changed
   he looked like a tree
      with bits and pieces of her
      hanging from his branches.

It made her smile
   seeing him in charge of all her things.
   She knew they were safe
      and so was she.

She remembered the lighthouse woman.
   She was there
     in him
     in them.

     Mercy.

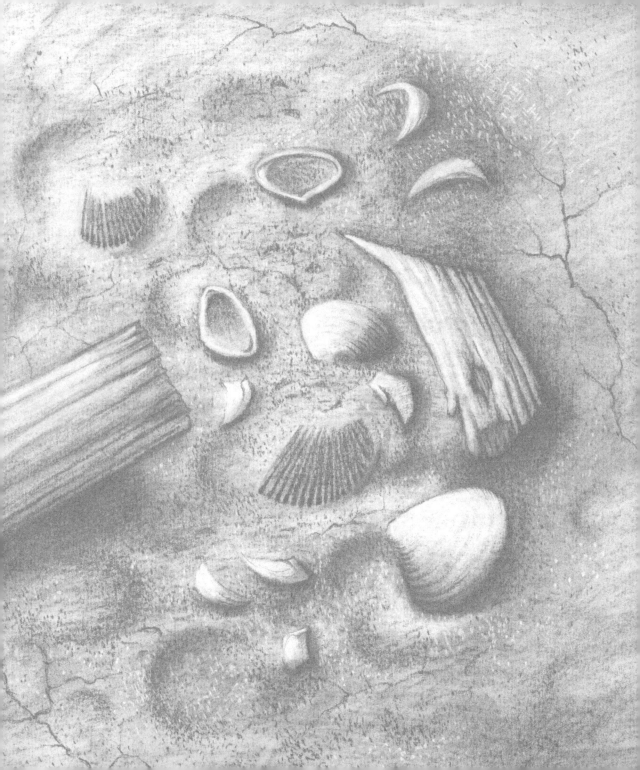

She awoke in a post-surgery haze
    disoriented
groggy.

What was this room
    with the sharp lights
    and strange noises;
    these needles and tubes?

When did this day begin?

She felt confused
    and terribly thirsty.

Then she heard someone saying her name.

There was a nurse
    sitting by her side
    helping her to awaken.

Then she realized where she was and why.

She turned to the nurse and asked,
    ''There's no more baby?''

and the nurse replied,
    ''No, honey, the baby's gone.''

The tears stung in her eyes
    and began to fall down her face
    but her arms were at her sides
        hindered by IVs
        and blood pressure cuffs
        and tucked under blankets.

The nurse bent over her
    and gently wiped the tears
        from her nose
        and her cheeks
            and spoke to her softly.

And then the nurse took chips of ice
    and put them one by one on her tongue.

Nothing had ever tasted so good.

    Mercy.

And she began to know what Sophia,
the lighthouse woman,
had told her.

She knew God.

*I*n the days that followed
    she felt the presence of God
        in herself
        in everything around her:

In rubbing her face against her daughter's
        as they cuddled in bed
        and she tried to explain what had happened.

In the tenderness of her family and friends
        the spring flowers that filled her house
        the shared tears
        the beginnings of laughter
        the joy of children

and the love that came to her so freely in her pain.

She felt that mercy in communion with many women
   some close friends
   others whom she hardly knew
    who shared their losses
     of infertility
     of pregnancies
     of babies.

She knew that mercy
   in experiencing the paradox
    of feeling her strength
     at a time when she felt most broken.

And slowly she began to know
    what the lighthouse keeper had told her.

She understood about the seasons of the beach:
    that the sweet warm gentle weather
        must alternate
        with the fierce and powerful storms.

In its own way,
        each gives something to the beach.

She understood about the beach house:
    that its beauty is in its durability
    and that its durability comes
    not from offering resistance to the power of the ocean
    but in finding a way for the water to pass through
        thereby saving it
        and letting it stand strong.

She understood about the sea glass:
    that tears and sorrow are as natural as the sea

  and that the cool green light of the glass
     doesn't come without cost

that what changes it from
    a worthless bit of discarded glass
       involves getting knocked around
         in the sand
         and the rocks

    and letting the ocean smooth over the jagged edges
      patiently
      slowly
      over a long, long time

so that one day
    a child walking on a New England beach
      will see a green light
      sparkling on the shore

      and she will bend down,
      pick it from the rocks
      and claim it as her treasure.

And in that moment the transformation is complete.

The sea's sorrow becomes the child's joy

and that is the mercy of God.

Sophia brings up her own children,
and cares for those who seek her.
Whoever loves her loves life,
those who wait on her early will be filled with happiness.
Whoever holds her close will inherit honor,
and wherever they walk the Lord will bless them.
Those who serve Sophia minister to the Holy One,
and the Lord loves those who love her.
Whoever obeys her judges aright,
and whoever pays attention to her dwells secure.
If they trust themselves to Sophia, they will inherit her,
and their descendants will remain in possession of her;
for though Sophia takes them at first through winding ways,
bringing fear and faintness to them,
plaguing them with her discipline until she can trust them,
and testing them with her ordeals,
in the end Sophia will lead them back to the straight road,
and reveal her secrets to them.

(see Ecclesiasticus 4:11-18)